◈

# NECESSITIES
# OF
# LIFE

# NECESSITIES OF LIFE

# POEMS

# 1962-1965

# Adrienne Rich

W · W · NORTON & COMPANY · INC ·

NEW YORK

Thanks are due to the following periodicals in which some of the poems first appeared: *Hudson Review, Maryland English Journal, The Nation, New York Review of Books, Paris Review, Poetry.* "Mourning Picture" was read as the Phi Beta Kappa poem at Swarthmore College in June, 1965. "I Am in Danger—Sir—" was first published as an epigraph to *Emily Dickinson: The Mind of the Poet* by Albert J. Gelpi (Harvard University Press, 1965) under the title "E."

SBN   393   04247   2   Cloth Edition

SBN   393   04269   9   Paper Edition

# ◈ CONTENTS

## PART TWO: TRANSLATIONS FROM THE DUTCH

◈

# PART ONE
◈

# POEMS
◈

# 1962-1965

Changeray-je pas pour vous cette belle
contexture des choses? C'est la condition
de vostre creation, c'est une partie de
vous que la mort: vous vous fuyez vous-
mesmes.

*Montaigne*

# ◆ NECESSITIES OF LIFE

Piece by piece I seem
to re-enter the world: I first began

a small, fixed dot, still see
that old myself, a dark-blue thumbtack

pushed into the scene,
a hard little head protruding

from the pointillist's buzz and bloom.
After a time the dot

begins to ooze. Certain heats
melt it.
                    Now I was hurriedly

blurring into ranges
of burnt red, burning green,

whole biographies swam up and
swallowed me like Jonah.

Jonah! I was Wittgenstein,
Mary Wollstonecraft, the soul

of Louis Jouvet, dead
in a blown-up photograph.

Till, wolfed almost to shreds,
I learned to make myself

unappetizing. Scaly as a dry bulb
thrown into a cellar

I used myself, let nothing use me.
Like being on a private dole,

sometimes more like kneading bricks in Egypt.
What life was there, was mine,

now and again to lay
one hand on a warm brick

and touch the sun's ghost
with economical joy,

now and again to name
over the bare necessities.

So much for those days. Soon
practice may make me middling-perfect, I'll

dare inhabit the world
trenchant in motion as an eel, solid

as a cabbage-head. I have invitations:
a curl of mist steams upward

from a field, visible as my breath,
houses along a road stand waiting

like old women knitting, breathless
to tell their tales.

1962

# IN THE WOODS

"Difficult ordinary happiness,"
no one nowadays believes in you.
I shift, full-length on the blanket,
to fix the sun precisely

behind the pine-tree's crest
so light spreads through the needles
alive as water just
where a snake has surfaced,

unreal as water in green crystal.
Bad news is always arriving.
"We're hiders, hiding from something bad,"
sings the little boy.

Writing these words in the woods,
I feel like a traitor to my friends,
even to my enemies.
The common lot's to die

a stranger's death and lie
rouged in the coffin, in a dress
chosen by the funeral director.
Perhaps that's why we never

see clocks on public buildings any more.
A fact no architect will mention.
We're hiders, hiding from something bad
most of the time.

Yet, and outrageously, something good
finds us, found me this morning
lying on a dusty blanket
among the burnt-out Indian pipes

and bursting-open lady's-slippers.
My soul, my helicopter, whirred

distantly, by habit, over
the old pond with the half-drowned boat

toward which it always veers
for consolation: ego's Arcady:
leaving the body stuck
like a leaf against a screen.—

Happiness! how many times
I've stranded on that word,
at the edge of that pond; seen
as if through tears, the dragon-fly—

only to find it all
going differently for once
this time: my soul wheeled back
and burst into my body.

Found! ready or not.
If I move now, the sun
naked between the trees
will melt me as I lie.

1963

## THE CORPSE-PLANT

(Whitman: *How can an obedient man, or a sick man, dare to write poems?*)

A milk-glass bowl hanging by three chains
from the discolored ceiling
is beautiful tonight. On the floor, leaves, crayons,
innocent dust foregather.

Neither obedient nor sick, I turn my head,
feeling the weight of a thick gold ring
in either lobe. I see the corpse-plants
clustered in a hobnailed tumbler

at my elbow, white as death, I'd say,
if I'd ever seen death;
whiter than life
next to my summer-stained hand.

Is it in the sun that truth begins?
Lying under that battering light
the first few hours of summer
I felt scraped clean, washed down

to ignorance. The gold in my ears,
souvenir of a shrewd old city,
might have been wearing thin as wires
found in the bones of a woman's head

miraculously kept in its essentials
in some hot cradle-tomb of time.
I felt my body slipping through
the fingers of its mind.

Later, I slid on wet rocks,
threw my shoes across a brook,
waded on algae-furred stones
to join them. That day I found

the corpse-plants, growing like
shadows on a negative
in the chill of fern and lichen-rust.
That day for the first time

I gave them their deathly names—
or did they name themselves?—
not "Indian pipes" as once
we children knew them.

Tonight, I think of winter,
winters of mind, of flesh,
sickness of the rot-smell of leaves
turned silt-black, heavy as tarpaulin,

obedience of the elevator cage
lowering itself, crank by crank
into the mine-pit,
forced labor forcibly renewed—

but the horror is dimmed:
like the negative of one
intolerable photograph
it barely sorts itself out

under the radiance of the milk-glass shade.
Only death's insect whiteness
crooks its neck in a tumbler
where I placed its sign by choice.

1963

## THE TREES

The trees inside are moving out into the forest,
the forest that was empty all these days
where no bird could sit
no insect hide
no sun bury its feet in shadow
the forest that was empty all these nights
will be full of trees by morning.

All night the roots work
to disengage themselves from the cracks
in the veranda floor.
The leaves strain toward the glass
small twigs stiff with exertion
long-cramped boughs shuffling under the roof
like newly discharged patients
half-dazed, moving
to the clinic doors.

I sit inside, doors open to the veranda
writing long letters
in which I scarcely mention the departure
of the forest from the house.
The night is fresh, the whole moon shines
in a sky still open
the smell of leaves and lichen
still reaches like a voice into the rooms.
My head is full of whispers
which tomorrow will be silent.

Listen. The glass is breaking.
The trees are stumbling forward
into the night. Winds rush to meet them.
The moon is broken like a mirror,
its pieces flash now in the crown
of the tallest oak.

1963

◆ LIKE THIS TOGETHER
for A.H.C.

### 1

Wind rocks the car.
We sit parked by the river,
silence between our teeth.
Birds scatter across islands
of broken ice. Another time
I'd have said "Canada geese,"
knowing you love them.
A year, ten years from now
I'll remember this—
this sitting like drugged birds
in a glass case—
not why, only that we
were here like this together.

### 2

They're tearing down, tearing up
this city, block by block.
Rooms cut in half
hang like flayed carcasses,
their old roses in rags,
famous streets have forgotten
where they were going. Only
a fact could be so dreamlike.
They're tearing down the houses
we met and lived in,
soon our two bodies will be all
left standing from that era.

### 3

We have, as they say,
certain things in common.
I mean: a view
from a bathroom window

over slate to stiff pigeons
huddled every morning; the way
water tastes from our tap,
which you marvel at, letting
it splash into the glass.
Because of you I notice
the taste of water,
a luxury I might
otherwise have missed.

4

Our words misunderstand us.
Sometimes at night
you are my mother:
old detailed griefs
twitch at my dreams, and I
crawl against you, fighting
for shelter, making you
my cave. Sometimes
you're the wave of birth
that drowns me in my first
nightmare. I suck the air.
Miscarried knowledge twists us
like hot sheets thrown askew.

5

Dead winter doesn't die,
it wears away, a piece of carrion
picked clean at last,
rained away or burnt dry.
Our desiring does this,
make no mistake, I'm speaking
of fact: through mere indifference
we could prevent it.
Only our fierce attention
gets hyacinths out of those
hard cerebral lumps,
unwraps the wet buds down
the whole length of a stem.

1963

## BREAKFAST IN A BOWLING ALLEY
## IN UTICA, NEW YORK

Smudged eyeballs,
mouth stale as air,
I'm newly dead, a corpse

so fresh the grave unnerves me.
Nobody here but me
and Hermes behind the counter

defrosting sandwich steaks.
Paeans of *vox humana*
sob from the walls. THIS LAND

IS MY LAND. . . . It sounds
mummified. Has no sex,
no liquor license.

I chew meat and bread
thinking of wheatfields—
a gold-beige ceinture—

and cattle like ghosts
of the buffalo, running
across plains, nearing

the abbatoir. Houses
dream old-fashionedly
in backwoods townships

while the land glitters
with temporary life
stuck fast by choice:

trailers put out taproots
of sewage pipe, suckers
of TV aerial—

but in one of them,
perhaps, a man
alone with his girl

for the first time.

1963

# ◈ OPEN-AIR MUSEUM

Ailanthus, goldenrod, scrapiron, what makes you flower?
What burns in the dump today?

Thick flames in a grey field, tended
by two men: one derelict ghost,
one clearly apter at nursing destruction,
two priests in a grey field, tending the flames
of stripped-off rockwool, split
mattresses, a caved-in chickenhouse,
mad Lou's last stack of paintings, each a perfect black lozenge

seen from a train, stopped
as by design, to bring us
face to face with the flag of our true country:
violet-yellow, black-violet,
its heart sucked by slow fire
O my America
this then was your desire?

but you cannot burn fast enough:
in the photograph the white
skirts of the Harlem bride
are lashed by blown scraps, tabloid sheets,
and her beauty a scrap of flickering light
licked by a greater darkness

This then was your desire!
those trucked-off bad dreams
outside the city limits
crawl back in search of you, eyes
missing, skins missing, intenser in decay
the carriage that wheeled the defective baby
rolls up on three wheels

and the baby is still inside,
you cannot burn fast enough
Blue sparks of the chicory flower
flash from embers of the dump
inside the rose-rust carcass of a slaughtered Chevrolet
crouches the young ailanthus

and the two guardians go raking the sacred field, raking
slowly, to what endless end
Cry of truth among so many lies
at your heart burns on
a languid fire

1964

# ✧ TWO SONGS

1.

Sex, as they harshly call it,
I fell into this morning
at ten o'clock, a drizzling hour
of traffic and wet newspapers.
I thought of him who yesterday
clearly didn't
turn me to a hot field
ready for plowing,
and longing for that young man
piercéd me to the roots
bathing every vein, etc.
All day he appears to me
touchingly desirable,
a prize one could wreck one's peace for.
I'd call it love if love
didn't take so many years
but lust too is a jewel
a sweet flower and what
pure happiness to know
all our high-toned questions
breed in a lively animal.

2.

That "old last act"!
And yet sometimes
all seems post coitum triste
and I a mere bystander.
Somebody else is going off,
getting shot to the moon.
Or, a moon-race!
Split seconds after
my opposite number lands

I make it—
we lie fainting together
at a crater-edge
heavy as mercury in our moonsuits
till he speaks—
in a different language
yet one I've picked up
through cultural exchanges . . .
we murmur the first moonwords:
*Spasibo. Thanks. O.K.*

1964

## ◈ THE PARTING

The ocean twanging away there
and the islands like scattered laundry—

You can feel so free, so free,
standing on the headland

where the wild rose never stands still,
the petals blown off

before they fall
and the chicory nodding

blue, blue, in the all-day wind.
Barbed wire, dead at your feet,

is a kind of dune-vine,
the only one without movement.

Every knot is a knife
where two strands tangle to rust.

1963

# NIGHT-PIECES: FOR A CHILD

## THE CRIB

You sleeping I bend to cover.
Your eyelids work. I see
your dream, cloudy as a negative,
swimming underneath.
You blurt a cry. Your eyes
spring open, still filmed in dream.
Wider, they fix me—
—death's head, sphinx, medusa?
You scream.
Tears lick my cheeks, my knees
droop at your fear.
Mother I no more am,
but woman, and nightmare.

## HER WAKING

Tonight I jerk astart in a dark
hourless as Hiroshima,
almost hearing you breathe
in a cot three doors away.

You still breathe, yes—
and my dream with its gift of knives,
its murderous hider and seeker,
ebbs away, recoils

back into the egg of dreams,
the vanishing point of mind.
All gone.

But you and I—
swaddled in a dumb dark
old as sickheartedness,
modern as pure annihilation—

we drift in ignorance.
If I could hear you now
mutter some gentle animal sound!
If milk flowed from my breast again. . . .

1964

# THE STRANGER

Fond credos, plaster ecstasies!
We arrange a prison-temple

for the weak-legged little god
who might stamp the world to bits

or pull the sky in like a muslin curtain.
We hang his shrine with bells,

aeolian harps, paper windmills,
line it with biscuits and swansdown.

His lack of culture we expected,
scarcely his disdain however—

that wild hauteur, as if
it were we who blundered.

Wildness we fret to avenge!
Eye that hasn't yet blinked

on the unblinking gold archways
of its trance—*that* we know

must be trained away:
that aloof, selective stare.

Otherness that affronts us
as cats and dogs do not—

once this was original sin
beaten away with staves of holy writ.

Old simplemindedness. But the primal fault
of the little god still baffles.

All other strangers are forgiven
their strangeness, but he—

how save the eggshell world from his
reaching hands, how shield

ourselves from the disintegrating
blaze of his wide pure eye?

1964

## ◇ AFTER DARK

### I

You are falling asleep and I sit looking at you
old tree of life
old man whose death I wanted
I can't stir you up now.

Faintly a phonograph needle
whirs round in the last groove
eating my heart to dust.
That terrible record! how it played

down years, wherever I was
in foreign languages even
over and over, *I know you better
than you know yourself* I know

*you better than you know
yourself* I know
*you* until, self-maimed,
I limped off, torn at the roots,

stopped singing a whole year,
got a new body, new breath,
got children, croaked for words,
forgot to listen

or read your *mene tekel* fading on the wall,
woke up one morning
and knew myself your daughter.
Blood is a sacred poison.

Now, unasked, you give ground.
We only want to stifle
what's stifling us already.
Alive now, root to crown, I'd give

—oh,—something—not to know
our struggles now are ended.
I seem to hold you, cupped
in my hands, and disappearing.

When your memory fails—
no more to scourge my inconsistencies—
the sashcords of the world fly loose.
A window crashes

suddenly down. I go to the woodbox
and take a stick of kindling
to prop the sash again.
I grow protective toward the world.


II

Now let's away from prison—
Underground seizures!
I used to huddle in the grave
I'd dug for you and bite

my tongue for fear it would babble
—Darling—
I thought they'd find me there
someday, sitting upright, shrunken,

my hair like roots and in my lap
a mess of broken pottery—
wasted libation—
and you embalmed beside me.

No, let's away. Even now
there's a walk between doomed elms
(whose like we shall not see much longer)
and something—grass and water—

and old dream-photograph.
I'll sit with you there and tease you
for wisdom, if you like,
waiting till the blunt barge

bumps along the shore.
Poppies burn in the twilight
like smudge pots.
I think you hardly see me

but—this is the dream now—
your fears blow out,
off, over the water.
At the last, your hand feels steady.

1964

# ◆ MOURNING PICTURE

(The picture is by Edwin Romanzo Elmer, 1850–1923)

They have carried the mahogany chair and the cane rocker
out under the lilac bush,
and my father and mother darkly sit there, in black clothes.
Our clapboard house stands fast on its hill,
my doll lies in her wicker pram
gazing at western Massachusetts.
This was our world.
I could remake each shaft of grass
feeling its rasp on my fingers,
draw out the map of every lilac leaf
or the net of veins on my father's
grief-tranced hand.

Out of my head, half-bursting,
still filling, the dream condenses—
shadows, crystals, ceilings, meadows, globes of dew.
Under the dull green of the lilacs, out in the light
carving each spoke of the pram, the turned porch-pillars,
under high early-summer clouds,
I am Effie, visible and invisible,
remembering and remembered.

They will move from the house,
give the toys and pets away.
Mute and rigid with loss my mother
will ride the train to Baptist Corner,
the silk-spool will run bare.
I tell you, the thread that bound us lies
faint as a web in the dew.
Should I make you, world, again,
could I give back the leaf its skeleton, the air
its early-summer cloud, the house
its noonday presence, shadowless,
and leave *this* out? I am Effie, you were my dream.

1965

◈ "I AM IN DANGER—SIR—"

"Half-cracked" to Higginson, living,
afterward famous in garbled versions,
your hoard of dazzling scraps a battlefield,
now your old snood

mothballed at Harvard
and you in your variorum monument
equivocal to the end—
who are you?

Gardening the day-lily,
wiping the wine-glass stems,
your thought pulsed on behind
a forehead battered paper-thin,

you, woman, masculine
in single-mindedness,
for whom the word was more
than a symptom—

a condition of being.
Till the air buzzing with spoiled language
sang in your ears
of Perjury

and in your half-cracked way you chose
silence for entertainment,
chose to have it out at last
on your own premises.

1964

# HALFWAY
### in memory: M.G.J.

In the field the air writhes, a heat-pocket.
Masses of birds revolve, blades
of a harvester.
The sky is getting milkily white,
a sac of light is ready to burst open.

Time of hailstones and rainbow.
My life flows North. At last I understand.
A young girl, thought sleeping, is certified dead.
A tray of expensive waxen fruit,
she lies arranged on the spare-room coverlid.

To sit by the fire is to become another woman,
red hair charring to grey,
green eyes grappling with the printed page,
voice flailing, flailing the uncomprehending.
My days lie open, listening, grandmother.

1965

# ◈ AUTUMN SEQUENCE

### 1.

An old shoe, an old pot, an old skin,
and dreams of the subtly tyrannical.
Thirst in the morning; waking into the blue

drought of another October
to read the familiar message nailed
to some burning bush or maple.

Breakfast under the pines, late yellow-
jackets fumbling for manna on the rim
of the stone crock of marmalade,

and shed pine-needles drifting
in the half-empty cup.
Generosity is drying out,

it's an act of will to remember
May's sticky-mouthed buds
on the provoked magnolias.

### 2.

Still, a sweetness hardly earned
by virtue or craft, belonging
by no desperate right to me

(as the marmalade to the wasp
who risked all in a last euphoria
of hunger)

washes the horizon. A quiet
after weeping, salt still on the tongue
is like this, when the autumn planet

looks me straight in the eye
and straight into the mind
plunges its impersonal spear:

*Fill and flow over, think*
*till you weep, then sleep*
*to drink again.*

3.

Your flag is dried-blood, turkey-comb
flayed stiff in the wind,
half-mast on the day of victory,

anarchist prince of evening marshes!
Your eye blurs in a wet smoke,
the stubble freezes under your heel,

the cornsilk *Mädchen* all hags now,
their gold teeth drawn,
the milkweeds gutted and rifled,

but not by you, foundering hero!
The future reconnoiters in dirty boots
along the cranberry-dark horizon.

Stars swim like grease-flecks
in that sky, night pulls a long knife.
Your empire drops to its knees in the dark.

4.

Skin of wet leaves on asphalt.
Charcoal slabs pitted with gold.
The reason for cities comes clear.

There must be a place, there has come a time—
where so many nerves are fusing—
for a purely moral loneliness.

Behind bloodsoaked lights of the avenues,
in the crystal grit of flying snow,
in this water-drop bulging at the taphead,

forced by dynamos three hundred miles
from the wild duck's landing and the otter's dive,
for three seconds of quivering identity.

There must be a place. But the eyeball stiffens
as night tightens and my hero passes out
with a film of stale gossip coating his tongue.

1964

# ◈ NOON

Light pulses through underground chambers.
I have to tell myself: my eyes are not blue.
Two dark holes
feed at the sky.

It swirls through them, raging
in azure spirals.
Nothing changes them:
two black tubes, draining off

a lake of iris.
Cleave open my skull:
the gouts of blue
leap from the black grotto.

1965

◈ NOT LIKE THAT

It's so pure in the cemetery.
The children love to play up here.
It's a little town, a game of blocks,
a village packed in a box,
a pre-war German toy.
The turf is a bedroom carpet:
heal-all, strawberry flower
and hillocks of moss.
To come and sit here forever,
a cup of tea on one's lap
and one's eyes closed lightly, lightly,
perfectly still
in a nineteenth-century sleep!
it seems so normal to die.

Nobody sleeps here, children.
The little beds of white wrought iron
and the tall, kind, faceless nurse
are somewhere else, in a hospital
or the dreams of prisoners of war.
The drawers of this trunk are empty,
not even a snapshot
curls in a corner.

In Pullmans of childhood we lay
enthralled behind dark-green curtains,
and a little lamp burned blue
all night, for us. The day
was a dream too, even the oatmeal
under its silver lid, dream-cereal
spooned out in forests of spruce
skirting the green-black gorges,
thick woods of sleep, half prickle,
half lakes of fern.
To stay here forever

is not like that, nor even
simply to lie quite still,
the warm trickle of dream
staining the thick quiet.
The drawers of this trunk are empty.
They are all out of sleep up here.

1965

◇ THE KNOT

In the heart of the queen anne's lace, a knot of blood.
For years I never saw it,

years of metallic vision,
spears glancing off a bright eyeball,

suns off a Swiss lake.
A foaming meadow; the Milky Way;

and there, all along, the tiny dark-red spider
sitting in the whiteness of the bridal web,

waiting to plunge his crimson knifepoint
into the white apparencies.

Little wonder the eye, healing, sees
for a long time through a mist of blood.

1965

# ◈ ANY HUSBAND TO ANY WIFE

*"Might I die last and show thee!"*

I know: you are glycerine,
old quills, rose velvet,
tearstains in *Middlemarch*,
a style of getting into cabs, of eating fruit,
a drawer of stones, chains, seeds, shells, little mirrors:
Darling, you will outlive yourself, and me.

Sometimes the sea backs up against a
lashed pier, grinding and twisting,
a turmoil of wrecked stuff
alive and dead. And the pier stands groaning
as if the land depended on it.
We say it is the moon that draws these tides,
then glazes in aftercalm
the black, blurred face to something we can love.

1965

## ◈ SIDE BY SIDE

Ho! in the dawn
how light we lie

stirring faintly as laundry
left all night on the lines.

You, a lemon-gold pyjama,
I, a trousseau-sheet, fine

linen worn paper-thin in places,
worked with the maiden monogram.

Lassitude drapes our folds.
We're slowly bleaching

with the days, the hours, and the years.
We are getting finer than ever,

time is wearing us to silk,
to sheer spiderweb.

The eye of the sun, rising, looks in
to ascertain how we are coming on.

1965

## ◈ SPRING THUNDER

**1.**

Thunder is all it is, and yet
my street becomes a crack in the western hemisphere,
my house a fragile nest of grasses.

The radiotelescope flings its nets
at random; a child is crying,
not from hunger, not from pain,
more likely impotence. The generals are sweltering

in the room with a thousand eyes.
Red-hot lights flash off and on
inside air-conditioned skulls.

Underfoot, a land-mass
puffed-up with bad faith and fatigue
goes lumbering onward,

old raft in the swollen waters,
unreformed Huck and Jim
watching the tangled yellow shores
rush by.

**2.**

Whatever you are that weeps
over the blistered riverbeds
and the cracked skin of cities,
you are not on our side,

eye never seeking our eyes,
shedding its griefs like stars
over our hectic indifference,
whispered monologue

subverting space with its tears,
mourning the mournable,
nailing the pale-grey woolly flower
back to its ledge.

3.

The power of the dinosaur
is ours, to die
inflicting death,
trampling the nested grasses:

power of dead grass
to catch fire
power of ash
to whirl off the burnt heap

in the wind's own time.

4.

A soldier is here, an ancient figure,
generalized as a basalt mask.

Breathes like a rabbit, an Eskimo,
strips to an older and simpler thing.

No criminal, no hero; merely a shadow
cast by the conflagration

that here burns down or there leaps higher
but always in the shape of fire,

always the method of fire, casting
automatically, these shadows.


5.

Over him, over you, a great roof is rising,
a great wall: no temporary shelter.
Did you tell yourself these beams would melt,

these fiery blocs dissolve?
Did you choose to build this thing?
Have you stepped back to see what it is?

It is immense; it has porches, catacombs.
It is provisioned like the Pyramids, for eternity.
Its buttresses beat back the air with iron tendons.

It is the first flying cathedral,
eating its parishes by the light of the moon.
It is the refinery of pure abstraction,

a total logic, rising
obscurely between one man
and the old, affective clouds.

1965

## MOTH HOUR

Space mildews at our touch.
The leaves of the poplar, slowly moving—
aren't they moth-white, there in the moonbeams?
A million insects die every twilight,
no one even finds their corpses.
Death, slowly moving among the bleached clouds,
knows us better than we know ourselves.

I am gliding backward away from those who knew me
as the moon grows thinner and finally shuts its lantern.
I can be replaced a thousand times,
a box containing death.
When you put out your hand to touch me
you are already reaching toward an empty space.

1965

# FOCUS
### for Bert Dreyfus

Obscurity has its tale to tell.
Like the figure on the studio-bed in the corner,

out of range, smoking, watching and waiting.
Sun pours through the skylight onto the worktable

making of a jar of pencils, a typewriter keyboard
more than they were. Veridical light . . .

Earth budges. Now an empty coffee-cup,
a whetstone, a handkerchief, take on

their sacramental clarity, fixed by the wand
of light as the thinker thinks to fix them in the mind.

O secret in the core of the whetstone, in the five
pencils splayed out like fingers of a hand!

The mind's passion is all for singling out.
Obscurity has another tale to tell.

1965

# FACE TO FACE

Never to be lonely like that—
the Early American figure on the beach
in black coat and knee-breeches
scanning the didactic storm in privacy,

never to hear the prairie wolves
in their lunar hilarity
circling one's little all, one's claim
to be Law and Prophets

for all that lawlessness,
never to whet the appetite
weeks early, for a face, a hand
longed-for and dreaded—

How people used to meet!
starved, intense, the old
Christmas gifts saved up till spring,
and the old plain words,

and each with his God-given secret,
spelled out through months of snow and silence,
burning under the bleached scalp; behind dry lips
a loaded gun.

1965

◈

# PART TWO
◈
# TRANSLATIONS FROM
◈
# THE DUTCH

These translations are from a group commissioned by the Bollingen Foundation. For criticism and linguistic advice my thanks go to Judith Herzberg, Marjan DeWolff, and Leo Vroman; the final responsibility is of course my own. The original Dutch poems will be found at the end of the group of translations.

*Martinus Nijhoff*

◈ THE SONG OF THE FOOLISH BEES

A smell of further honey
embittered nearer flowers,
a smell of further honey
sirened us from our meadow.

That smell and a soft humming
crystallized in the azure,
that smell and a soft humming,
a wordless repetition,

called upon us, the reckless,
to leave our usual gardens,
called upon us, the reckless,
to seek mysterious roses.

Far from our folk and kindred
joyous we went careering,
far from our folk and kindred
exhuberantly driven.

No one can by nature
break off the course of passion,
no one can by nature
endure death in his body.

Always more fiercely yielding,
more lucently transfigured,
always more fiercely yielding
to that elusive token,

we rose and staggered upward,
kidnapped, disembodied,
we rose and vanished upward,
dissolving into glitter.

It's snowing; we are dying,
homeward, downward whirled.
It's snowing; we are dying;
it snows among the hives.

*Hendrik de Vries*

◈ MY BROTHER

My brother, nobody knows
the end you suffered.
Often you lie beside me, dim, and I
grow confused, grope, and startle.

You walked along that path through the elms.
Birds cried late. Something wrong
was following us both. But you
wanted to go alone through the waste.

Last night we slept again together.
Your heart jerked next to me. I spoke your name
and asked where you were going.
Your answer came:
"The horror! . . . there's no telling . . .
"See: the grass
"lies dense again, the elms
"press round."

*Hendrick de Vries*

◈ FEVER

Listen! It's never sung like that! Listen!
The wallpaper stirred,
and the hairs of the heavy-fringed eye.
What flew
through the rooms?

Tomorrow it will be
as if all night the whips
hadn't lashed so.—
                    See, through the blinds,
the spirits in their cold ships!

Boughs graze the frame
of the window. Far off, a whistle
sounds, always clearly, along the fields.
The beasts on the walls
fade away. The light goes out.

Gerrit Achterberg

◈
EBEN HAËZER

(Hebrew for "Stone of Help"; a common old name
for farmhouses in Holland)

Sabbath evening privacy at home.
Mist-footsteps, prowling past the shed.
At that hour, not another soul abroad;
the blue farmhouse a closed hermitage.

There we lived together, man and mouse.
Through cowstall windows an eternal fire
fell ridged from gold lamps on the threshing-floor,
stillness of linseed cakes and hay in house.

There my father celebrated mass:
serving the cows, priestlike at their heads.
Their tongues curled along his hands like fish.

A shadow, diagonal to the rafters.
Worship hung heavy from the loftbeams.
His arteries begin to calcify.

*Gerrit Achterberg*

◈ ACCOUNTABILITY

Old oblivion-book, that I lay open.
White eye-corner rounding the page.

Gold lace slips out under the evening,
Green animals creep backwards.

Lifelessness of the experimental station.
Added-up, subtracted sum.

Black night. Over the starlight skims
God's index finger, turning the page.

Death comes walking on all fours
past the room, a crystal egg,

with the lamp, the books, the bread,
where you are living and life-size.

◈ STATUE

A body, blind with sleep,
stands up in my arms.
Its heaviness weighs on me.
Death-doll.
I'm an eternity too late.
And where's your heartbeat?

The thick night glues us together,
makes us compact with each other.
"For God's sake go on holding me—
my knees are broken,"
you mumble against my heart.

It's as if I held up the earth.
And slowly, moss is creeping
all over our two figures.

*Leo Vroman*

◈ OUR FAMILY

My father, who since his death
no longer speaks audibly
lies sometimes, a great walrus
from nightfall to daybreak
his muzzle in my lap
in the street from his chin down.


The light of morning feeds
through his hide, thinned to parchment,
and his slackened features dwindle
to a line creeping off among the chairs;
if I rise to peer at him
he winces away to a dot.


In the daytime there's nothing to see
but an emphatically vanished
absence where moments ago
the sun too was just shining.


Where my father has stood
it now just quivers,
rippling by handfuls through
my little daughter's light hair
while on the sunny grass
she slowly scampers forward.


Her little snoot is so open
you could easily spread it out
with a teaspoon or your finger
on a slice of fresh white bread
or, if need be,
you could mould it into a pudding.

Her little voice itches like a fleece;
it wriggles gaily into my ear
and can't get out when it laughs;
with plopping fishfins
it folds itself struggling up
into my head. Where it spends the night.

And here, this taller child
is Tineke, my wife.
She hums a nursery rhyme
to the hair on her third breast,
which whimpers, being a baby,
and a thirsty baby at that.

I have such a gentle family,
it kisses, goes on eight legs,
but it has no moustache:
my father has vanished,

and they too are all going to die:
too soft, if they turn into air,
to swing a weathercock;
if turned into water, too slight
to fill a gutter; if into light
to make one live cock crow.

*Chr. J. van Geel*

◈ HOMECOMING

The sea, a body of mysterious calls
is almost motionless.
I know a beach, a tree stands there
in which women are singing,
voluptuous, languid.

In harbors ships are steaming
full of honey from the sea. Drizzle hangs
like eyelashes over the landscape.

Behind the seadike, breathing invisibly
in the mist, sleep the cows.
The hobble of a horse drags along the fence,
holding still where I stand with sweet words.

Listen, the sea calls,
claps her hands.
The ships running out in the wet
come like children—one drags
a sled into the garden.

◈ SLEEPWALKING
     (next to death)

                 Sleep, horns of a snail

    Out of the black and white bed, floors of red glaze,
    mornings in the careful garden
    on paths suitable rubbish slowly buried
    and without urgency overgrown with grass
    with ivy and sometimes a flower
    just as we dream
    to see unseen, to listen unattended.

             The twigs of the moon
             in indifferent white,
             horns upright, wood with-
             out leaf and seeking bees,
             sadness down to the ground.

Like silence always and from afar
lisps the water
never, by no one possessed.

             Dead trees in green leaf.
             What to do but among bushes,
             what to see but underbrush.

On this sun time sharpens itself
to brilliance.

A stone of untouchable fire
on which time breaks its tooth.

Time caught no hour: loafing next to
a blaze.

In the darkened town the old groped
                    with their sticks.
The rays of the sun are tired,
the beetles rot in the wood,
only the sea. . . .
In the earth of the dead
earth covers leaf, leaf covers leaf.

Heartbeat of the wild creeper,
hammer between wing-lashes,
butterflies hammer at the sun.

Now you must get to the institution
with a mask on, your little feet
tarred, an iron crown on your head.

You awake there a python,
a boa constrictor,
after seven-and-twenty years,
after six-and-twenty years,
fair sleep, fair sleepers.

You strike the prince twice
a youth wasted with waiting
for your serpent eyes and
you unfold your scaly tail.

Now you must get to the institution
with a mask on, your little feet
tarred, an iron crown on your head.

Night blows away from the sun,
sky in fresh wind,
the sea kicks off its surf.

The moon scorches, a cloud of steam.
Driving water torn to shreds,
sunny twilight, fruitless field.

Tamed sea, muscular
to the temples, stoop where no coast
is, under the familiar blows,
stand where you cannot stand,
night is embraced on the sun.

A scared hind in a wood of one tree.

Whether the dead live, how they rest or
decay, leaves me cold, for cold for good and all
is death.

Poor is the frontier of life, to die blossoms
away over the graves.

Every existence competes in every
lost chance of life for death.

Of always fewer chances, one moved
and drove over her, naked standing by her child
death.

Residing in a thunderstorm,
sky hoists sun, night cuts light.
The wind's wings are at home.

Whistle now out of the nights
sparks of burnt paper.
Whisper fire in the days
dried by the sun, your desires
are lightened, curled to ash.

Flowers for hunger,

the darkest, the blue,
of ash, of grey granite,
black ice,

room without window,
abacus without beads,
room without a person,
the eaten past
gnaws,
the teeth out of the comb,
the funeral wreath emptily devoured,
a stone.

Whatever I may contrive—
and I contrive it—death's
private roads are the coldest night.

That I shall not be with her—
not with her—
that nothing shall glimmer
except danger.

Trees of ash, trees of ice,
the light frozen.
Summer and winter are
constructed of one emptiness.
The boughs of the wind are dead.

Must I dejected and contemplating death
now that above the sea a cloudless night
empties the sky, let treason and false laughter
prudently ring out until the morning?

the threshold of the horizon shifts—
and think with the thinkers of this earth:
"Life is thus"—then am I crazed
because my heart encloses what it held?

Morning has broken and the sea
is wide, I go back home to sleep.
Path, dune, trees and sheep
are rosy from the east, a rosy gull
flies up under the rash sky.
What's silent speaks aloud buried in sleep.

*Martinus Nijhoff*

❖ HET LIED DER DWAZE BIJEN

Een geur van hoger honing
verbitterde de bloemen,
een geur van hoger honing
verdreef ons uit de woning.

Die geur en een zacht zoemen
in het azuur bevrozen,
die geur en een zacht zoemen
een steeds herhaald niet-noemen,

riep ons, ach roekelozen,
de tuinen op te geven,
riep ons, ach roekelozen,
naar raadselige rozen

Ver van ons volk en leven
zijn wij naar avonturen
ver van ons volk en leven
jubelend voortgedreven.

Niemand kan van nature
zijn hartstocht onderbreken,
niemand kan van nature
in lijve de dood verduren.

Steeds heviger bezweken,
steeds helderder doorschenen,
steeds heviger bezweken
naar het ontwijkend teken,

stegen wij en verdwenen,
ontvoerd, ontlijfd, ontzworven
stegen wij en verdwenen
als glinsteringen henen.—

Het sneeuwt, wij zijn gestorven,
huiswaarts omlaag gedwereld,
het sneeuwt, wij zijn gestorven,
het sneeuwt tussen de korven.

*Hendrik De Vries*

### ◈ MIJN BROER

Mijn broer, gij leedt
Een einde, waar geen mensch van weet.
Vaak ligt gij naast mij, vaag, en ik
Begrijp het slecht, en tast en schrik.

De weg met iepen liept gij langs.
De vogels riepen laat. Iets bangs
Vervolgde ons beiden. Toch woudt gij
Alleen gaan door de woestenij.

Wij sliepen deze nacht weer saam.
Uw hart sloeg naast mij. 'k Sprak uw naam
En vroeg, waarheen gij gingt.
Het antwoord was:
". . . Te vreeselijk om zich in te verdiepen.
"Zie: 't Gras
"Ligt weder dicht met iepen
"Omkringd."

### ◈ KOORTS

Hoor! Zoo is nooit gezongen! Hoor!
't Behang bewoog,
En 't haar van 't zwaarbewimperd oog.
Wat vloog
De ruimten door?

't Zal morgen zijn
Of 't niet bij nacht zoo hard met zweepen
Geslagen had.—
      Zie door 't gordijn
De geesten in hun koude schepen!

De takken schaven aan de randen
Van 't venster. In de verte fluit
Het altijd helder langs de landen.
De dieren op de wanden
Verdwijnen. 't Licht gaat uit.

*Gerrit Achterberg*

◈
## EBEN HAËZER

Besloten zaterdagavond bij ons thuis.
Mistvoeten liepen sluipend langs de schuur.
Er was geen ziel meer buiten op dat uur;
de blauwe boerderij een dichte kluis.

Daar woonden wij bijeen met man en muis.
Door koestalraampjes viel een richel vuur
uit goudlampen cp deel, eeuwig van duur
en stil van lijnkoeken en hooi in huis.

Mijn vader celebreerde er de mis:
de koeien voeren, plechtig bij de koppen.
Hun tong krult om zijn handen als een vis.

Een schim, diagonaal tot in de nokken.
Godsdienst hing zwaar tegen de hanebalken.
Zijn aderen beginnen te verkalken.

*Gerrit Achterberg*

◈ COMPTABILITEIT

Oud vergeetboek, dat ik opensla.
Witte ooghoek om de pagina.

Goudgalon, onder de avond uit.
Groene dieren kruipen achteruit.

Levenloosheid van het proefstation.
Opgetelde, afgetrokken som.

Zwarte nacht. Over de sterren scheert
Gods wijsvinger, die het blad omkeert.

Op zijn handen komt de dood voorbij
aan de kamer, een kristallen ei,

met de lamp, de boeken en het brood,
waar gij levend zijt en levensgroot.

◈ STANDBEELD

Een lichaam, blind van slaap,
staat in mijn armen op.
Ik voel hoe zwaar het gaat.
Dodepop.
Ik ben een eeuwigheid te laat.
Waar is je harteklop?

De dikke nacht houdt ons bijeen
en maakt ons met elkaar compact.
"Om Gods wil laat mij niet meer los;
mijn benen zijn geknakt,"
fluister je aan mijn borst.

Het is of ik de aarde tors.
En langzaam kruipt het mos
over ons standbeeld heen.

*Leo Vroman*

## ONS GEZIN

Mijn vader, die sinds zijn dood
niet meer hoorbaar praat,
ligt soms, als een walrus zo groot,
van de nacht tot de dageraad
met zijn knevel in mijn schoot
en vanaf zijn kin op straat.

In de morgen vreet dan het licht
door zijn huid, tot een vlies verdund,
en slinkt zijn verslapt gezicht
tot een lijn die tussen de stoelen wegkruipt,
als ik mij turend opricht
krimpt hij ineen tot een punt.

Overdag is er niets te zien
dan een met nadruk verdwenen
afwezigheid waar voordien
de zon ook al had geschenen.

Waar mijn vader heeft gestaan
waait het alleen maar.
Handenvol vleugen gaan
door mijn dochtertjes lichte haar
terwijl zij op het zonnige gras
langzaam voortholt.

Haar snuitje is zo bloot,
met een theelepeltje of een vinger
is het makkelijk uit te spreiden
op een lapje vers wit brood,
of, in geval van nood,
als een papje te bereiden.

Haar stemmetje jeukt als een vacht;
het wriemelt mijn oor graag binnen;
het kan er niet uit als het lacht;
met plappende visjesvinnen
vouwt het zich scharrelend op
in mijn hoofd. Waar het overnacht.

En hier, dit langere kind,
is Tineke, mijn vrouw.
Zij zingt een kinderliedje
tot het haar op haar derde borst,
welke kreunt, want dat is een babietje,
en dat babietje heeft dorst.

Ik heb zulk een zacht gezin,
het zoent en heeft acht benen,
maar er zit geen knevel in:
mijn vader is verdwenen,

en zij gaan ook allemaal dood;
als lucht zullen ze dan wel zacht waaien,
geen weerhaan kunnen doen draaien,
en als water een enkele dakgoot
nauwelijks vullen: als licht
geen levende haan doen kraaien.

*Chr. J. van Geel*

◈ THUISKOMEN

De zee, een lijf van geheimzinnig roepen,
beweegt haast niet.
Ik ken een strand, er staat een boom
waarin de vrouwen zingen,
wellustig, loom.

In havens liggen schepen onder stoom
vol honing van de zee. Motregen hangt
als wimpers voor het landschap.

Achter de zeedijk, ademend en in de mist
ontzichtbaar, slapen de koeien.
De kluister van een paard sleept naar het hek toe,
houdt stil waar ik met zoete woorden sta.

Hoor, de zee roept,
klapt in haar handen.
De scheepjes stuivend in het nat
komen als kinderen—een sleept
een slee het tuintje in.

Chr. J. *van Geel*

◈ SLAAPWANDELEN
(naast de dood)

Slaap, horens van een slak

Uit het zwart en witte bed, de vloeren van rood lak,
's ochtends in de voorzichtige tuin,
op paden geschikt puin langzaam begraven
en zonder dringen overgroeid door gras,
door klimop en een enkele bloem,
zoals wij dromen,
zien ongezien, luisteren onbeluisterd.

De takken van de maan
in onverschillig wit,
horens rechtop, hout zon-
der blad en zoekende bijen,
verdriet tot op de grond.

Als stilte steeds en van verweg
lispelt het water
van niemand ooit geweest.

Dode bomen in groen blad.
Wat te doen dan tussen struiken,
wat te zien dan struikgewas.

Aan deze zon slijpt zich de tijd
briljant.

Een steen van onhanteerbaar vuur
waar tijd zijn tand op brak.

Tijd ving geen uur: straatslijpen naast
een brand.

In de verduisterde stad tastten de ouden met hun stok.
De stralen van de zon zijn moe,
de torren rotten in het hout,
alleen de zee. . . .
In de aarde der gestorvenen
dekt aarde, blad de bladeren toe.

Hartslag van de wingerd,
hamer tussen vleugels—wimpers,
vlinders timmeren aan de zon.

Nu moet je naar het gesticht,
een masker voor, je voetjes
geteerd, een ijzer kroontje op.

Je ontwaakt er als python,
als boa konstriktor,
na zevenentwintig jaar,
na zesentwintig jaar
schoon slapen, schone slaapsters.

Je slaat de prins tweemaal
een jeugd verdaan met wachten
je slangeogen op en
je ontvouwt je schubbestaart.

Nu moet je naar het gesticht,
een masker voor, je voetjes
geteerd, een ijzer kroontje op.

De nacht waait van de zon,
hemel in frisse wind,
de zee woelt branding bloot.

De maan schroeit, een wolk van stoom.
Gescheurd het drijvend water,
zonnige schemer, vruchteloos veld.

Getemde zee, gespierd
tot op de slaap, buk waar geen kust
is onder de eigen slagen,
sta waar je niet kan staan,
de nacht wordt op de zon omhelsd.

Een bang ree in een bos van één boom

Of doden leven, hoe zij rusten of
vergaan, mij laat het koud, want koud voorgoed
is dood.

Arm is de grens van leven, sterven bloeit
over de graven heen.

Ieder bestaan dingt in iedere
verkeken kans op leven naar de dood.

Van altijd mindar kansen één bewoog
en dreef over haar naakt staan naast haar kind
de dood.

Gevestigd in een onweer hijst
de hemel zon, de nacht snijdt licht.
De vleugels van de wind zijn thuis.

Fluit nu uit de nachten
vonken van verbrand papier.
Fluister vuur de dagen in
door de zon verdroogd, je wensen
zijn verlicht tot as gekruld.

Bloemen voor de honger,

de donkerste, de blauwe,
van as, van grijs graniet,
zwart ijs,
een kamer zonder raam,
een telraam zonder kralen,
een kamer zonder mens,
gegeten knaagt de tijd
voorbij,
de tanden uit de kam,
de grafkrans leeggeschranst,
een steen.

Wat ik ook verzinnen mag—
en ik verzin het—doods
eigen wegen zijn de koudste nacht.

Dat ik met haar niet zijn zal,
niet met haar,
dat geen schijnsel zijn zal
dan gevaar.

Bomen van as, bomen van ijs,
het licht bevroren.
Zomer en winter zijn
gemetseld van dezelfde leegte.
De takken van de wind zijn dood.

Moet ik mistroostig en den dood betrachtend,
nu boven zee een wolkeloze nacht
de hemel leegt, verraad en valse lach
voorzichtig klinken laten tot de ochtend

de drempel van de horizon verzet
en denken met de denkenden op aarde:
'zo is het leven'—maar ben ik dan gek
omdat mijn hart omsluit wat het bewaarde?

De ochtend is gekomen en de zee
is wijd, ik ga naar huis om te gaan slapen.
Het pad, het duin, de bomen en de schapen
zijn roze van het oosten, roze meeuw
onder de roekeloze hemel stijgt.
Verzwegen in de slaap klinkt mee wat zwijgt.

# NOTES ON THE POEMS

# PART ONE

"In the Woods"—The first line is borrowed and translated from the Dutch poet, J. C. Bloem.

"Mourning Picture"—Effie is the painter's daughter, who died young, and the speaker of the poem.

"I Am In Danger—Sir—" See *The Letters of Emily Dickinson*, T. H. Johnson, ed., Vol. II, p. 409.

"Any Husband to Any Wife"—The title is, of course, a reversal of Browning's, and the epigraph comes from his poem.

PART TWO

Anyone who will compare the Dutch poems with my translations will see that I have, deliberately, refrained from imitating rhyme patterns and have in some instances altered metres. I have tried to be faithful first of all to the images and the emotional tone of the poems, and have been unwilling to introduce distortions in order to reproduce formal structure. Much of the onomatopoeic music of the Nijhoff poem is thus necessarily lost. Possibly I have made Hendrik de Vries sound more modern than he actually sounds in Dutch: in "My Brother" for instance he uses an old form of the second person singular which corresponds to the English "thou." But I believe that the inner structure of these poems remains in the translations, and as a poet-translator I have tried to do as I would be done by.